My Very Own Big Spanish Dictionary

Mi gran diccionario de español

By the Editors of the American Heritage® Dictionaries

Illustrated by Pamela Zagarenski

Houghton Mifflin Company

Boston • New York

Visit our website: www.houghtonmifflinbooks.com

Library of Congress Cataloging-in-Publication Data
My very own big Spanish dictionary = Mi gran diccionario de español / by the editors of the
American Heritage dictionaries ; illustrated by Pamela Zagarenski.- - 1st ed.
    p. cm.
 ISBN-13: 978-0-618-62126-2
 ISBN-10: 0-618-62126-1
1. Picture dictionaries, Spanish- -Juvenile literature. 2. English language- -Dictionaries,
Juvenile- -Spanish. I. Title: Mi gran diccionario de español. II. Zagarenski, Pamela.
 PC4629.M98 2005
 423'.61- -dc22

                          2005015911

Manufactured in Singapore

TWP 10 9 8 7 6 5 4 3

airplane
el avión

alligator
el caimán

ambulance
la ambulancia

ant
la hormiga

apple
la manzana

astronaut
el astronauta

Bb

baby
el bebé

ball
la pelota
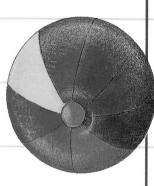

baker
el panadero

balloon
el globo

banana
la banana

band
el conjunto

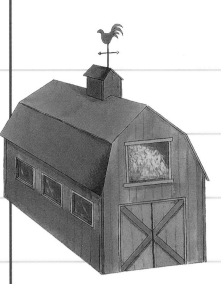

barn
el granero

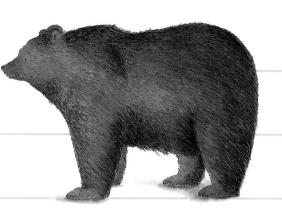

bear
el oso

book
el libro

boy
el niño

bus
el autobús

butterfly
la mariposa

Cc

cactus
el cactus

camel
el camello

car
el coche

carrot
la zanahoria

castle
el castillo

cat
el gato

chair
la silla

clock
el reloj

cold
tener frío

computer
la computadora

cook
cocinar

cow
la vaca

cry
llorar

Dd

dig
cavar

dinosaur
el dinosaurio

dog
el perro

dolphin
el delfín

draw
dibujar

dragon
el dragón

8

eagle
el águila

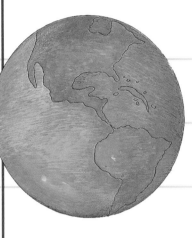

Earth
la Tierra

eat
comer

egg
el huevo

elephant
el elefante

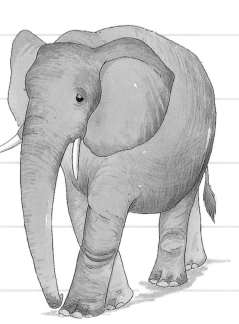

Ff

farmer
el granjero

fish
el pez

firefighter
el bombero

frog
la rana

flower
la flor

garden
el huerto

giraffe
la jirafa

girl
la niña

goldfish
el pececillo de color

grasshopper
el saltamontes

goose
el ganso

helicopter
el helicóptero

hop
brincar

horse
el caballo

hot
tener calor

house
la casa

hug
abrazar

ice cream
el helado

ice-skate
patinar sobre hielo

igloo
el iglú

jacket
la chaqueta

juggle
hacer juegos malabares

jump
saltar

Kk

kangaroo
el canguro

kick
patear

king
el rey

kite
la cometa

knock
llamar a la puerta

koala
el koala

**ladybug
la mariquita**

**laugh
reír**

**lighthouse
el faro**

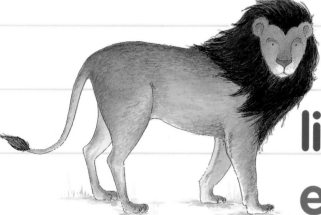

**lion
el león**

**lizard
el lagarto**

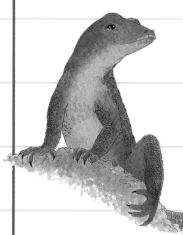

**lobster
la langosta**

mailbox
el buzón

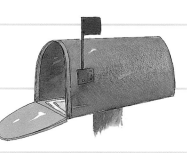

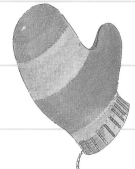

mitten
el mitón

man
el hombre

moose
el ante

monkey
el mono

mouse
el ratón

nest
el nido

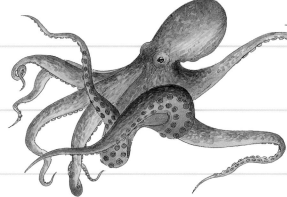

octopus
el pulpo

night
la noche

onion
la cebolla

orange
la naranja

owl
el búho

Pp

panda
el panda

parade
el desfile

parrot
el loro

penguin
el pingüino

pie
el pastel

pig
el cerdo

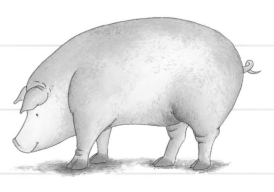

porcupine
el puerco espín

pour
verter

pull
tirar de

pumpkin
la calabaza

push
empujar

Qq

queen
la reina

question mark
el signo de interrogación

quiet
callarse

quilt
la colcha

rabbit
el conejo

read
leer

rhinoceros
el rinoceronte

robot
el robot

rooster
el gallo

run
correr

Ss

sailboat
el barco de vela

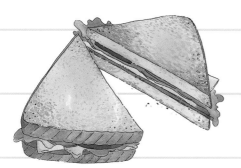

sandwich
el sándwich

scarecrow
el espantapájaros

scratch
rascar

shadow
la sombra

shark
el tiburón

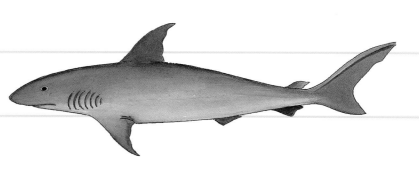

sing
cantar

sleep
dormir

snow
la nieve

soccer
el fútbol

sun
el sol

swim
nadar

Tt

talk
hablar
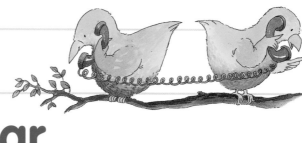

telescope
el telescopio

throw
lanzar
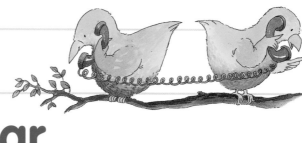

tie
atar
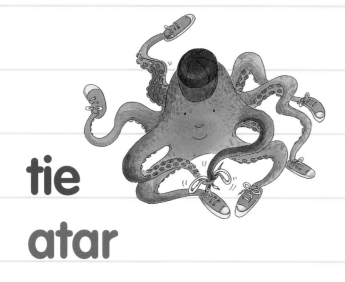

tiger
el tigre

tornado
el tornado

umbrella
el paraguas

unicorn
el unicornio

uniform
el uniforme

van
la furgoneta

violin
el violín

volcano
el volcán

Ww

wash
lavarse

wet
mojado

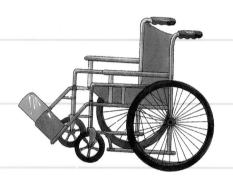

whale
la ballena

wheelchair
la silla de ruedas

woman
la mujer

write
escribir

x-ray
la radiografía

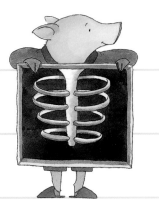

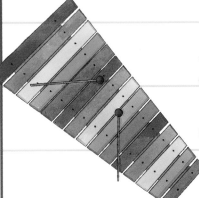

xylophone
el xilófono

yard
el jardín

yo-yo
el yoyó

zebra
la cebra

zoo
el zoo

Index/Índice

For the purpose of presenting the Spanish index in alphabetical order, each word appears without its article.

A

	abrazar hug	12
	águila eagle	9
	ambulancia ambulance	3
	ante moose	16
	astronauta astronaut	3
	atar tie	24
	autobús bus	5
	avión airplane	3

B

	ballena whale	26
	banana banana	4
	barco de vela sailboat	22
	bebé baby	4
	bombero firefighter	10

	brincar hop	12
	búho owl	17
	buzón mailbox	16

C

	caballo horse	12
	cactus cactus	6
	caimán alligator	3
	calabaza pumpkin	19
	callarse quiet	20
	camello camel	6
	canguro kangaroo	14
	cantar sing	23
	casa house	12
	castillo castle	6

	cavar dig	8
	cebolla onion	17
	cebra zebra	27
	cerdo pig	18
	chaqueta jacket	13
	coche car	6
	cocinar cook	7
	colcha quilt	20
	comer eat	9
	cometa kite	14
	computadora computer	7
	conejo rabbit	21
	conjunto band	4
	correr run	21
D	**delfín** dolphin	8

	desfile parade	18
	dibujar draw	8
	dinosaurio dinosaur	8
	dormir sleep	23
	dragón dragon	8
E	**elefante** elephant	9
	empujar push	19
	escribir write	26
	espantapájaros scarecrow	22
F	**faro** lighthouse	15
	flor flower	10
	furgoneta van	25
	fútbol soccer	23
G	**gallo** rooster	21
	ganso goose	11

29

	Spanish	English	Page
	gato	cat	6
	globo	balloon	4
	granero	barn	5
	granjero	farmer	10
H	**hablar**	talk	24
	hacer juegos malabares	juggle	13
	helado	ice cream	13
	helicóptero	helicopter	12
	hombre	man	16
	hormiga	ant	3
	huerto	garden	11
	huevo	egg	9
I	**iglú**	igloo	13
J	**jardín**	yard	27
	jirafa	giraffe	11

	Spanish	English	Page
K	**koala**	koala	14
L	**lagarto**	lizard	15
	langosta	lobster	15
	lanzar	throw	24
	lavarse	wash	26
	leer	read	21
	león	lion	15
	libro	book	5
	llamar a la puerta	knock	14
	llorar	cry	7
	loro	parrot	18
M	**manzana**	apple	3
	mariposa	butterfly	5
	mariquita	ladybug	15
	mitón	mitten	16

	mojado wet	26
	mono monkey	16
	mujer woman	26

N

	nadar swim	23
	naranja orange	17
	nido nest	17
	nieve snow	23
	niña girl	11
	niño boy	5
	noche night	17

O

	oso bear	5

P

	panadero baker	4
	panda panda	18
	paraguas umbrella	25
	pastel pie	18

	patear kick	14
	patinar sobre hielo ice-skate	13
	pececillo de color goldfish	11
	pelota ball	4
	perro dog	8
	pez fish	10
	pingüino penguin	18
	puerco espín porcupine	19
	pulpo octopus	17

R

	radiografía x-ray	27
	rana frog	10
	rascar scratch	22
	ratón mouse	16
	reina queen	20
	reír laugh	15

	reloj clock	7
	rey king	14
	rinoceronte rhinoceros	21
	robot robot	21
S	**saltamontes** grasshopper	11
	saltar jump	13
	sándwich sandwich	22
	signo de interrogación question mark	20
	silla chair	7
	silla de ruedas wheelchair	26
	sol sun	23
	sombra shadow	22
T	**telescopio** telescope	24
	tener calor hot	12
	tener frío cold	7

	tiburón shark	22
	Tierra Earth	9
	tigre tiger	24
	tirar de pull	19
	tornado tornado	24
U	**unicornio** unicorn	25
	uniforme uniform	25
V	**vaca** cow	7
	verter pour	19
	violín violin	25
	volcán volcano	25
X	**xilófono** xylophone	27
Y	**yoyó** yo-yo	27
Z	**zanahoria** carrot	6
	zoo zoo	27

Activities/Actividades

1 Identify the things in different groups found in the book, such as the foods, animals, and methods of transportation.

Identifique las cosas que hay en los diferentes grupos que aparecen en el libro, por ejemplo: comestibles, animales y medios de transporte.

2 Pose a question or make a statement and let the child find the answer and say the word in both English and Spanish. For example:

Plantee una pregunta o haga una declaración, y deje que el niño encuentre la respuesta y diga la palabra en inglés y en español. Por ejemplo:

- What fruit is red?/¿Qué fruta es roja?

- Can you find an animal that lives in a desert climate?/¿Puedes encontrar un animal que viva en un clima del desierto?

- What would melt if not eaten quickly?/¿Qué se derretiría si no se come rápidamente?

- What sea animal has eight tentacles?/¿Qué animal marino tiene ocho tentáculos?

- What would you make to scare away birds from your garden?/¿Qué harías para asustar a los pájaros de tu huerto?

- What do you open and hold to keep from getting wet when it rains?/¿Qué abres y sostienes para evitar que te mojes cuando llueve?

- It can fly in the sky on a string./Puede volar en el cielo atado de una cuerda.

- It has claws that pinch!/¡Tiene garras que pellizcan!

- The mail carrier might leave letters for you in this./El cartero podría dejar las cartas para ti en esto.

- They keep your hands warm in the winter./Mantienen tus manos calientes en el invierno.

- To serve milk from a pitcher, you would do this./Para servir leche de una jarra, harías esto.

- You can look through this for a close-up view of the moon and stars at night./Puedes mirar con esto para observar más de cerca la luna y las estrellas por la noche.

3 Give a word in English or Spanish and have the child find the corresponding illustration. Ask the child to say the word in the other language.

Dé una palabra en inglés o español y haga que el niño encuentre la ilustración correspondiente. Pídale al niño que diga la palabra en el otro idioma.

4 Select three (or more) illustrations from the book and construct a story incorporating those entries, substituting the Spanish word for the illustration each time that word is mentioned in the story. To get you started:

Seleccione tres (o más) ilustraciones del libro y cree una historia que las incluya, substituyendo la palabra en inglés con la ilustración cada vez que se mencione la palabra en la historia. Para comenzar:

- apple, baker, pie/manzana, panadero, pastel

- dig, garden, scarecrow/cavar, huerto, espantapájaros

- carrot, garden, rabbit/zanahoria, huerto, conejo

- barn, cow, owl/granero, vaca, búho

- book, night, sleep/libro, noche, dormir

- camel, ice cream, sun/camello, helado, sol

- castle, dragon, king, queen/castillo, dragón, rey, reina

- cold, mitten, ice-skate, snow/frío, mitón, patinar sobre hielo, nieve

5 Say a page number in English or Spanish and instruct the child to go to that page. The art on that page starts with what letter?

Diga el número de una página en inglés o en español y pídale al niño que vaya a esa página. ¿Con qué letra empieza el arte de esa página?

6 Point to a page in the book. Then instruct the child to go to the Numbers page in the back of the book. Instruct the child to point to the corresponding number and say the number in English and Spanish.

Señale una página del libro. Pídale al niño que vaya a la página de los números que está al final del libro. Pídale al niño que señale el número correspondiente y diga el número en inglés y en español.

7 Ask the child to point to an illustration. Then tell the child as much as you can about what is depicted.

Pídale al niño que señale una ilustración. Luego dígale todo lo que pueda sobre el dibujo.

If the child points to the apple, you can tell the child that apples

- are fruits
- grow on trees
- come in different varieties (sweet, tart) and colors (red, green, and yellow)
- can be eaten raw or cooked

Si el niño señala la manzana, usted puede decirle que las manzanas

- son frutas
- crecen en los árboles
- tienen diferentes variedades (dulces, ácidas) y colores (rojas, verdes y amarillas)
- pueden comerse crudas o cocidas

If the child points to the penguin, you can tell the child that penguins

- are a type of bird
- cannot fly, but are good swimmers
- walk upright on their two feet
- eat fish, shrimp, and squid

Si el niño señala el pingüino, usted puede decirle que los pingüinos

- son un tipo de pájaro
- no pueden volar, pero son buenos nadadores
- caminan verticalmente en sus dos patas
- comen peces, camarones y calamares

8 To invite additional discussion regarding these illustrations or others, you could make an observation about and ask questions relating to each object. For instance:

Para invitar a la charla adicional sobre estas ilustraciones u otras, podría hacer una observación al respecto y hacer preguntas referentes a cada objeto. Por ejemplo:

- An orange is a type of fruit. What other fruits can the child name? What color is each fruit named?

  La naranja es un tipo de fruta. ¿Qué otras frutas puede nombrar el niño? ¿De qué color es cada una de las frutas nombradas?

- Penguins live in a cold climate. Are there other animals that live in cold climates? Which animals live where it is very hot?

  Los pingüinos viven en climas fríos. ¿Hay otros animales que vivan en climas fríos? ¿Qué animales viven donde hace mucho calor?

- Many birds build their nests in trees. Where else might a bird build a nest?

  Muchos pájaros construyen los nidos en los árboles. ¿En qué otros lugares podrían construir su nido los pájaros?

- Birds live in nests. Where do dolphins (ants, tigers, etc.) live?

  Los pájaros viven en nidos. ¿Dónde viven los delfines (las hormigas, los tigres, etc.)?

Numbers/Números

0 zero **cero**	1 one **uno**	2 two **dos**	3 three **tres**	4 four **cuatro**
5 five **cinco**	6 six **seis**	7 seven **siete**	8 eight **ocho**	9 nine **nueve**
10 ten **diez**	11 eleven **once**	12 twelve **doce**	13 thirteen **trece**	14 fourteen **catorce**
15 fifteen **quince**	16 sixteen **dieciséis**	17 seventeen **diecisiete**	18 eighteen **dieciocho**	19 nineteen **diecinueve**
20 twenty **veinte**	21 twenty-one **veintiuno**	22 twenty-two **veintidós**	23 twenty-three **veintitrés**	24 twenty-four **veinticuatro**
25 twenty-five **veinticinco**	26 twenty-six **veintiséis**	27 twenty-seven **veintisiete**	28 twenty-eight **veintiocho**	29 twenty-nine **veintinueve**
30 thirty **treinta**	31 thirty-one **treinta y uno**	32 thirty-two **treinta y dos**	33 thirty-three **treinta y tres**	34 thirty-four **treinta y cuatro**
35 thirty-five **treinta y cinco**	36 thirty-six **treinta y seis**	37 thirty-seven **treinta y siete**	38 thirty-eight **treinta y ocho**	39 thirty-nine **treinta y nueve**
40 forty **cuarenta**	41 forty-one **cuarenta y uno**	42 forty-two **cuarenta y dos**	43 forty-three **cuarenta y tres**	44 forty-four **cuarenta y cuatro**
45 forty-five **cuarenta y cinco**	46 forty-six **cuarenta y seis**	47 forty-seven **cuarenta y siete**	48 forty-eight **cuarenta y ocho**	49 forty-nine **cuarenta y nueve**

55	56	57	58	59
fifty-five	fifty-six	fifty-seven	fifty-eight	fifty-nine
cincuenta y cinco	**cincuenta y seis**	**cincuenta y siete**	**cincuenta y ocho**	**cincuenta y nueve**
60	61	62	63	64
sixty	sixty-one	sixty-two	sixty-three	sixty-four
sesenta	**sesenta y uno**	**sesenta y dos**	**sesenta y tres**	**sesenta y cuatro**
65	66	67	68	69
sixty-five	sixty-six	sixty-seven	sixty-eight	sixty-nine
sesenta y cinco	**sesenta y seis**	**sesenta y siete**	**sesenta y ocho**	**sesenta y nueve**
70	71	72	73	74
seventy	seventy-one	seventy-two	seventy-three	seventy-four
setenta	**setenta y uno**	**setenta y dos**	**setenta y tres**	**setenta y cuatro**
75	76	77	78	79
seventy-five	seventy-six	seventy-seven	seventy-eight	seventy-nine
setenta y cinco	**setenta y seis**	**setenta y siete**	**setenta y ocho**	**setenta y nueve**
80	81	82	83	84
eighty	eighty-one	eighty-two	eighty-three	eighty-four
ochenta	**ochenta y uno**	**ochenta y dos**	**ochenta y tres**	**ochenta y cuatro**
85	86	87	88	89
eighty-five	eighty-six	eighty-seven	eighty-eight	eighty-nine
ochenta y cinco	**ochenta y seis**	**ochenta y siete**	**ochenta y ocho**	**ochenta y nueve**
90	91	92	93	94
ninety	ninety-one	ninety-two	ninety-three	ninety-four
noventa	**noventa y uno**	**noventa y dos**	**noventa y tres**	**noventa y cuatro**
95	96	97	98	99
ninety-five	ninety-six	ninety-seven	ninety-eight	ninety-nine
noventa y cinco	**noventa y seis**	**noventa y siete**	**noventa y ocho**	**noventa y nueve**
100	1,000	10,000	100,000	1,000,000
one hundred	one thousand	ten thousand	one hundred thousand	one million
cien	**mil**	**diez mil**	**cien mil**	**un millón**

white **blanco**	black **negro**	gray **gris**
brown **marrón**	yellow **amarillo**	orange **anaranjado**
purple **morado**	red **rojo**	pink **rosado**
green **verde**	blue **azul**	

Shapes/Formas

circle
el círculo

triangle
el triángulo

square
el cuadro

rectangle
el rectángulo

crescent
la crescent

diamond
el diamante

star
la estrella

oval
el óvalo

cone
el cono

cylinder
el cilindro

sphere
la esfera

pyramid
la pirámide

Which Illustration Does Not Belong?/¿Qué ilustración no pertenece?

banana
la banana

egg
el huevo

orange
la naranja

parrot
el loro

owl
el búho

panda
el panda

unicorn
el unicornio

dragon
el dragón

whale
la ballena

sailboat
el barco de vela

sing
cantar

band
el conjunto

ice-skate
patinar sobre hielo

x-ray
la radiografía

soccer
el fútbol

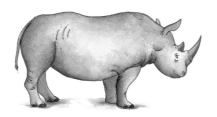

rhinoceros
el rinoceronte

whale
la ballena

dolphin
el delfín

helicopter
el helicóptero

clock
el reloj

kite
la cometa

octopus
el pulpo

porcupine
el puerco espín

cactus
el cactus

Put in Alphabetical Order/ Coloca en orden alfabético

ambulance
ambulancia

kangaroo
canguro

baker
panadero

tie
atar

pull
tirar de

clock
reloj

laugh
reír

draw
dibujar

wheelchair
silla de ruedas

volcano
volcán

wash
lavarse

mitten
mitón

onion
cebolla

knock
llamar a la puerta

soccer
fútbol

shadow
sombra

dog
perro

xylophone
xilófono

rooster
gallo

penguin
pingüino

throw
lanzar

eat
comer

frog
rana

dinosaur
dinosaurio

firefighter
bombero

pumpkin
calabaza

elephant
elefante

cook
cocinar

parrot
loro

igloo
iglú

jump
saltar

camel
camello

kick
patear

airplane
avión

butterfly
mariposa

horse
caballo

barn
granero

hug
abrazar

45

Days of the Week/
Días de la semana

June/**junio**

Sunday domingo	Monday lunes	Tuesday martes	Wednesday miércoles	Thursday jueves	Friday viernes	Saturday sábado
				1	2	3
4	5	6	7	8	9	10
11	12	13	14	15	16	17
18	19	20	21	22	23	24
25	26	27	28	29	30	

June/**junio**

Sunday domingo	Monday lunes	Tuesday martes	Wednesday miércoles	Thursday jueves	Friday viernes	Saturday sábado
				1	2	3
4	5	6	7	8	9	10
11	12	13	14	15	16	17
18	19	20	21	22	23	24
25	26	27	28	29	30	

June/**junio**

Sunday domingo	Monday lunes	Tuesday martes	Wednesday miércoles	Thursday jueves	Friday viernes	Saturday sábado
				1	2	3
4	5	6	7	8	9	10
11	12	13	14	15	16	17
18	19	20	21	22	23	24
25	26	27	28	29	30	

June/**junio**

Sunday domingo	Monday lunes	Tuesday martes	Wednesday miércoles	Thursday jueves	Friday viernes	Saturday sábado
				1	2	3
4	5	6	7	8	9	10
11	12	13	14	15	16	17
18	19	20	21	22	23	24
25	26	27	28	29	30	

June/**junio**

Sunday domingo	Monday lunes	Tuesday martes	Wednesday miércoles	Thursday jueves	Friday viernes	Saturday sábado
				1	2	3
4	5	6	7	8	9	10
11	12	13	14	15	16	17
18	19	20	21	22	23	24
25	26	27	28	29	30	

June/**junio**

Sunday domingo	Monday lunes	Tuesday martes	Wednesday miércoles	Thursday jueves	Friday viernes	Saturday sábado
				1	2	3
4	5	6	7	8	9	10
11	12	13	14	15	16	17
18	19	20	21	22	23	24
25	26	27	28	29	30	

June/**junio**

Sunday domingo	Monday lunes	Tuesday martes	Wednesday miércoles	Thursday jueves	Friday viernes	Saturday sábado
				1	2	3
4	5	6	7	8	9	10
11	12	13	14	15	16	17
18	19	20	21	22	23	24
25	26	27	28	29	30	

Months/Meses

January/enero

Sunday domingo	Monday lunes	Tuesday martes	Wednesday miércoles	Thursday jueves	Friday viernes	Saturday sábado
1	2	3	4	5	6	7
8	9	10	11	12	13	14
15	16	17	18	19	20	21
22	23	24	25	26	27	28
29	30	31				

February/febrero

Sunday domingo	Monday lunes	Tuesday martes	Wednesday miércoles	Thursday jueves	Friday viernes	Saturday sábado
		1	2	3	4	
5	6	7	8	9	10	11
12	13	14	15	16	17	18
19	20	21	22	23	24	25
26	27	28				

March/marzo

Sunday domingo	Monday lunes	Tuesday martes	Wednesday miércoles	Thursday jueves	Friday viernes	Saturday sábado
			1	2	3	4
5	6	7	8	9	10	11
12	13	14	15	16	17	18
19	20	21	22	23	24	25
26	27	28	29	30	31	

April/abril

Sunday domingo	Monday lunes	Tuesday martes	Wednesday miércoles	Thursday jueves	Friday viernes	Saturday sábado
						1
2	3	4	5	6	7	8
9	10	11	12	13	14	15
16	17	18	19	20	21	22
23	24	25	26	27	28	29
30						

May/mayo

Sunday domingo	Monday lunes	Tuesday martes	Wednesday miércoles	Thursday jueves	Friday viernes	Saturday sábado
	1	2	3	4	5	6
7	8	9	10	11	12	13
14	15	16	17	18	19	20
21	22	23	24	25	26	27
28	29	30	31			

June/junio

Sunday domingo	Monday lunes	Tuesday martes	Wednesday miércoles	Thursday jueves	Friday viernes	Saturday sábado
				1	2	3
4	5	6	7	8	9	10
11	12	13	14	15	16	17
18	19	20	21	22	23	24
25	26	27	28	29	30	

July/julio

Sunday domingo	Monday lunes	Tuesday martes	Wednesday miércoles	Thursday jueves	Friday viernes	Saturday sábado
						1
2	3	4	5	6	7	8
9	10	11	12	13	14	15
16	17	18	19	20	21	22
23	24	25	26	27	28	29
30	31					

August/agosto

Sunday domingo	Monday lunes	Tuesday martes	Wednesday miércoles	Thursday jueves	Friday viernes	Saturday sábado
		1	2	3	4	5
6	7	8	9	10	11	12
13	14	15	16	17	18	19
20	21	22	23	24	25	26
27	28	29	30	31		

September/septiembre

Sunday domingo	Monday lunes	Tuesday martes	Wednesday miércoles	Thursday jueves	Friday viernes	Saturday sábado
					1	2
3	4	5	6	7	8	9
10	11	12	13	14	15	16
17	18	19	20	21	22	23
24	25	26	27	28	29	30

October/octubre

Sunday domingo	Monday lunes	Tuesday martes	Wednesday miércoles	Thursday jueves	Friday viernes	Saturday sábado
1	2	3	4	5	6	7
8	9	10	11	12	13	14
15	16	17	18	19	20	21
22	23	24	25	26	27	28
29	30	31				

November/noviembre

Sunday domingo	Monday lunes	Tuesday martes	Wednesday miércoles	Thursday jueves	Friday viernes	Saturday sábado
		1	2	3	4	
5	6	7	8	9	10	11
12	13	14	15	16	17	18
19	20	21	22	23	24	25
26	27	28	29	30		

December/diciembre

Sunday domingo	Monday lunes	Tuesday martes	Wednesday miércoles	Thursday jueves	Friday viernes	Saturday sábado
					1	2
3	4	5	6	7	8	9
10	11	12	13	14	15	16
17	18	19	20	21	22	23
24	25	26	27	28	29	30
31						